A DOMESTIC CLIENT'S GUIDE
TO ENGAGING AN ARCHITECT

T0138972

RIBA ₩ Publishing

© RIBA Publishing, 2017

Published by RIBA Publishing, part of RIBA Enterprises Ltd, The Old Post Office, St Nicholas Street, Newcastle upon Tyne, NE1 1RH

ISBN 978-1-85946-765-7

The right of Nigel Ostime to be identified as the Author of this Work has been asserted in accordance with the Copyright, Designs and Patents Act 1988 sections 77 and 78.

British Library Cataloguing-in-Publication Data
A catalogue record for this book is available from the British Library.

Commissioning Editor: Elizabeth Webster
Project Editor: Daniel Culver
Production: Philip Handley
Designed by Kneath Associates
Typeset by Full Point Creative Media Ltd
Printed and bound by Page Bros, Norwich, UK

While every effort has been made to check the accuracy and quality of the information given in this publication, neither the Author nor the Publisher accept any responsibility for the subsequent use of this information, for any errors or omissions that it may contain, or for any misunderstandings arising from it.

www.ribaenterprises.com

CONTENTS

INTRODUCTION

The aims of this book are to:

— Improve project outcomes through a considered process of selection of the architect by the client

— Inform clients of the value architects can bring to their projects

— Provide best practice advice on, and a full understanding of, the legal requirements of the appointment process

— Provide clients with an explanation of the project process.

This guide can be used by architects to explain the project process to their clients and the role of the architect within that process. Architects may find it helpful to give a copy to their clients at the commencement of a project.

Please note that this book is intended for use by those who wish to build a new home, or extend or refurbish an existing one, for their own occupation or as a second home. If it is to be let you will be deemed a business client and you should refer instead to the sister publication to this book: *A Commercial Client's Guide to Engaging an Architect.*

FOREWORD

This book is an addition to the wealth of material which the Royal Institute of British Architects (RIBA) has developed to strengthen the client–architect relationship and improve project outcomes. The Institute has for some time now focused on clients as one of its core programmes through the 'RIBA for Clients' initiative, led by the Client Liaison Group, and that continues under my presidency.

The RIBA aims to champion better buildings, communities and the environment through architecture and our members. One way the institute can do this is by providing clients with the means to select the most appropriate architect for their project and inform them of the sort of questions they should be asking and what to expect during the project process.

This easily digestible but comprehensive guide provides the key information needed to engage the most appropriate architect for your project and to get the most value from the relationship. Make a few hours to read it and absorb the recommendations before you commence your project – it will be the most valuable time you spend on it.

Ben Derbyshire
RIBA President

PREFACE

I was pleased to be asked to update this publication because it ties in with the work of the RIBA Client Liaison Group that I have chaired since its inception in 2013. The group has conducted sector-focused roundtables, one-to-one filmed interviews and an online client satisfaction survey – the first of its kind in the industry, as well as other client-focused initiatives. Having more than 2,000 clients in our client database enabled us to develop and share unique insight into what it is that clients want from their architects. That data has been fed into this Guide and will help to improve outcomes on all projects.

There is considerable detail in the results of the survey which can be downloaded free of charge, along with a wealth of other information by searching 'client survey' at **www.architecture.com**.

We found that architects' designs are generally considered to be of high quality and meet (or exceed) the requirements of the brief. The process of managing projects has room for improvement and there is advice in this guide to achieve that. A significant but unsurprising finding was that qualified architects perform better than non-qualified designers on all counts.

The architectural profession has rightly been praised for turning the mirror on itself through the survey, showing maturity and a desire to achieve continuous improvement, and I hope this guide will continue in that vein and help us, through good client–architect dialogue, to achieve better outcomes on all projects.

With increasing use of the internet and comparison websites it is easier than ever to select the provider with the lowest price. However, consumers always have to be careful that they are comparing like with like, and this is particularly the case with professional services. Clients must take care in their selection processes because the choice of architect will have a profound effect on the outcome of the project. Cost is always an important factor but value and the level of service being provided must also be considered, especially where the investment has a long-term impact, as is the case when developing the built environment – be it a major project or a domestic extension.

Nigel Ostime

ACKNOWLEDGEMENTS

The author would like to thank Linda Stevens, Head of Client Services at the RIBA, whose drive and enthusiasm has been key to the Client Liaison Group since its inception and who has been an enormous help in producing this book. He would also like to thank Rob Earl, Client Services Manager at the RIBA, and the members of the Client Liaison Group, past and present, for their enthusiasm and ideas, and in particular Matt Thompson who has produced insightful articles disseminating our findings as well as the text for the case studies in this book. Thank you also to the architects and clients of the case studies. They have illuminated the narrative and lent it a real-life perspective. Finally, thanks to Paul Bussey and Peter Waxman for sharpening the chapter on CDM.

ABOUT THE AUTHOR

Nigel Ostime is an architect and Project Delivery Director at Hawkins\ Brown, a practice regarded for its people-focused approach and strong design ethos.

Nigel has wide experience in the design and delivery of projects ranging from multi-million pound developments to the domestic scale.

He is an active member of the RIBA, currently being a member of the Practice and Profession Committee and chair of the Client Liaison Group, which provides an interface between the institute and client bodies. He also sits on the RIBA Health and Safety steering group and set up the Future Leaders initiative, an education programme for business-focused, post-Part 3 skills for architects. He has been a member of the RIBA Plan of Work review group and the RIBA Professional Services Contract review group.

He has edited the last two editions of the *RIBA Job Book* (2008 and 2013) and the *Handbook of Practice Management* (2009 and 2013), and is author of the *Small Projects Handbook* (2014). He has developed two toolkits for RIBA members, one for quality management and the other for the briefing/evaluation process.

He lectures at Manchester, Westminster and The Bartlett schools of architecture and is a regular speaker at architecture and construction industry conferences on a range of topics

01

DO I NEED AN ARCHITECT?

Kevin McCloud,
developer and
TV presenter,
Grand Designs

"

A good architect actually pays for themselves – more than once. You will reap the reward and the building will be hugely better and deliver much better value for it. "

The process of designing and building or extending your most valuable asset is likely to be a nerve-racking experience. Unless your project is very simple, it makes sense to at least talk to an architect for advice before you get going.

Architects are highly skilled and professionally trained to turn your aspirations into reality. They will guide you through the design, planning and construction process whether you are constructing a new building or adapting an existing property.

Generally, architects begin to offer a full service for projects with a budget of £50,000 or more, but for a small one-off fee an architect can help you figure out how to get the best out of your project, regardless of size and whether they are needed later on. Most architects working on domestic projects offer these one-off consultations and they can be incredibly useful. They will give you guidance on all aspects of your project from design and cost through to planning and construction. In a short space of time you can gain an enormous amount of valuable information which will help you realise your project.

If you need planning permission it is sensible to engage an architect to take you at least up to that stage in the process. Your architect will help you with the approvals required before your project can go ahead, including the preparation of applications to the local authority for planning consent (where needed) and for Building Regulations approval.

Architects have a unique ability to see things from the widest possible perspective, as well as to also focus in on very small things that make the difference to the project.

A survey conducted by the *Architect's Journal* a few years ago found that what architects do is largely a mystery to the general public: 72 per cent of people did not know that architects apply for planning permission; 86 per cent didn't know that architects select, negotiate with and manage contractors; and quite astonishingly 15 per cent did not know that architects design buildings! So an important first step in answering the question 'Do I need an architect?' is to cover the basics. This guide will do that, as well as explaining how and where architects can add value and actually save cost.

Cost is always an issue and, as purchasers of goods and services our instinct is to pay the lowest price we find available in the market. But alongside cost it is important to also consider value. This is particularly the case with such long-term investments as property development, alteration and refurbishment.

An architect will be able to advise not just on how to optimise the capital construction cost, but also on minimising cost in use. This is important because the cost of maintaining and operating buildings through their life can be more than the construction cost.

Building projects are complicated and as a consequence carry risk and managing the risk is a value-adding exercise. They also obviously have to be done correctly first time. One of the great architects of the 20th century, Frank Lloyd Wright, famously said: 'A doctor can bury his mistakes but an architect can only advise his clients to plant vines'. Happily, the 2016 RIBA Working with Architects client satisfaction survey found that architects' design skills and ability to interpret and develop the brief are highly rated (78 per cent of clients were very or fairly satisfied with the aesthetic qualities of the project and 69 per cent of clients were very or fairly satisfied with the architect's ability to develop and interpret the brief). And with the ubiquitous rise of the use of 3D computer programmes, clients often now have the opportunity to experience a virtual building before the actual building is tendered.

Architects' training

Architects undergo five years of university education (an honours degree and two years of postgraduate study), plus two years of practical training before they are eligible to take their final professional exams. The title 'architect' is protected by law in the UK by the Architects Act 1997, so that only those who have undergone this rigorous training and are registered with the Architects Registration Board (ARB) are entitled to use it. Watch out for companies styling themselves as 'architectural' designers or similar wording, because this is generally an indication that they are not eligible. Only architects registered with the ARB are eligible to become members of the Royal Institute of British Architects (RIBA).

The five-year university training teaches architects how to interpret a brief and develop a range of design options that meet it, working with their client to find the one that best suits their aspirations. It also teaches thinking creatively, and developing the conceptual ideas into technical drawings and specifications to enable a building contractor to price and then construct the building. Architects also learn about the complicated town planning process; achieving a 'good' planning permission is an area where architects excel, often raising the value of the land by a multiple of their fee.

Architects apply impartial and creative thinking to projects large and small, whether you are constructing, adapting or expanding a building. They will guide you through the design, planning and construction process – from the early stage scenario of 'What do I do?' through to completion of the project.

Royal Institute of British Architects

The RIBA was established in 1834 and was granted its Royal Charter in 1837. It has 40,000 members worldwide and continues to perform its core remit of 'promoting and facilitating the acquirement of the knowledge of the various arts and sciences connected therewith'. The RIBA is a mark of quality. Architects who are members of the RIBA can call on a range of resources to broaden their knowledge that are not available to non-members.

Architectural practices can apply to become a RIBA Chartered Practice (see Chapter 9).

All RIBA Chartered Practices must have at least one of the principals and one in 10 of the employees in the firm being RIBA Chartered Members, and all project work must be supervised by a RIBA Chartered Member. Clients who have used a RIBA Chartered Practice will receive support from the RIBA should there be any disputes.

All architects comply with rigorous codes of conduct set by the ARB and the RIBA. This is covered in Chapter 10.

Insurance

All architects must be covered by a proportionate level of professional indemnity (PI) insurance that can be called on should it be required. This cover must be maintained for the duration of the liability period after completion – either six or twelve years, depending on the terms of their appointment.

What services can an architect provide?

Your architect can provide a range of services including:

— Investigating the feasibility of the requirements
— Developing design proposals
— Applying for statutory approvals
— Preparing construction information
— Obtaining tenders for building work
— Administering the building contract.

An architect works with a broad palette of skills and can provide or arrange other services connected with the project such as interior design, landscaping or making measured surveys of a site or building.

For more details on what architects do, see Chapter 6: Project process.

02

SELECTING AN ARCHITECT

es Bicknell,
rivate domestic
ient

"

The motivation for the project was to get the house to work. It used to be very hot in the summer and very cold in the winter. We wanted to solve the practical problems and create something beautiful in the process. What the architect brought was a recognition that the spaces we live in, the objects we engage with, affect our lives and good design affects it positively. Spaces should make you feel good. The environment that I live in now makes me feel good. "

Before contacting an architect, you will need to draw up the project brief. This is your wish list for the project. Focus on what you want to achieve, noting down all your requirements and highlighting any problems that need solving. Think in terms of how you will use the space now and in the future, rather than what needs to be built.

You should also try to establish your overall budget. This will help you to discuss costs up front with the architect and avoid disappointment at a later stage.

Once you have considered the brief and the budget, it is a good time to consult an architect. Most architects offer one-off consultations and these can be incredibly useful. During the consultation the architect will give you guidance on all the aspects of your project from design and cost, through to planning and construction. In a short space of time you can gain an enormous amount of valuable information which will help you realise your project.

Clients often appoint an architect who is known to them or who has been recommended, or whose work they admire. This can be a sound initial response, but a more structured process of selection is desirable where matching requirements with the range of skills and services available has to be more precise.

Look for a practice with experience of your type of project or one that shares your aspirations. Check how many similar projects they have built, their contacts with local authority town planners and their track record of approvals. Follow up their references too. Find out how responsive they were to changes and how effective they were at managing the budget.

You should first draw up a shortlist of practices. The RIBA can provide assistance on this (see Chapter 11: Find an Architect and Chapter 12: RIBA Competitions).

Contact each practice on your shortlist, describe your project and ask if they are available to accommodate it. If so, request literature that outlines the firm's qualifications and experience. Ask to see a portfolio of work, or to visit finished buildings, and visit their websites. Above all, talk to your intended architect. It is important to ensure that you are compatible. Your architect must convince you both of their creativity and their ability to get things done.

What to ask for

You may ask the architect to provide some or all of the following in addition to the proposed fees, schedule of services and so on:

— Previous examples of similar projects
— The team to undertake the project, including relevant curriculum vitae's (CVs)
— A method statement as to how the work will be undertaken
— Company policies on, for example, health and safety, quality control, sustainability, equal opportunities
— Qualifications held and awards won
— Confirmation of professional indemnity (PI) insurance and public and employer's liability insurance.

RIBA Client Services	The RIBA Client Services team can provide information and help you with your selection process free of charge. They can be contacted on 020 7307 3700, or email: **clientservices@riba.org**.

You can also make use of the RIBA Find an Architect online directory where you can create your own shortlist from over 3,000 RIBA Chartered Practices and 40,000 projects. Go to **www.architecture.com**.

Alternatively, you can speak to RIBA Client Services directly and they will create a tailored shortlist of practices with the appropriate skills and experience on your behalf. The service is confidential and provided free of charge.

See Chapter 11 for further information on this.

RIBA Competitions	For larger projects, a competition or competitive interview can be a successful way of selecting an architect. Competitions can help to drive up quality, stimulate creativity and innovation and generate a range of ideas to improve choice. The RIBA's dedicated Competitions Team provides a bespoke competition management service that is fair, transparent and well-structured, with a proven track record of success.

For more information on this service see Chapter 12.

A written appointment

A good working relationship between architect and client is crucial to the success of any project. You and your architect should discuss and agree on the scope and cost of architectural services before the project begins and ensure that the agreement is in writing.

The RIBA publishes the Domestic Professional Services Contract, which is suitable for use where the client requires work to their home.

For more information on appointments see Chapter 4.

03

HOW DO ARCHITECTS CHARGE THEIR FEES AND HOW MUCH ARE THEY?

Private domestic homeowner

"

Our architects cleverly remodelled our house to create amazing living spaces that we love. They really got to know us and listened to our ideas too. The end result is that we have beautiful spaces that work for our family. We're on phase two now – a really cool cabin in the garden. As a first time client, we had no idea what could be achieved through good design. Our house is now a home. "

Architects' fees will vary depending on the location and complexity of the project and the level of service. Some architects will charge you on the basis of a total project cost, others on a fixed-price lump sum or on a time-charge basis.

How much or how little you commission an architect is up to you – from an initial design discussion through to the final delivery of the project on site and even post-occupancy evaluation.

Architects will generally determine their fee proposal on the basis of an assessment of the anticipated cost of undertaking the work plus a level of profit. Your decision as to which architect to appoint should not be based on price alone, but should be an assessment of the value they will bring through the quality of their work and their skill and experience as a practitioner.

On receipt of an enquiry from a client, the architect will first need to decide whether, in principle, they wish to undertake the commission. In doing this they will be considering such matters as:

— Is the project likely to proceed?
— Does this project fit with the practice's established ambitions?
— If a competition, is it one the practice stands a reasonable chance of winning?
— Is the commission of a type in which the practice has expertise, or in which it wishes to gain expertise?
— Will the commission help enhance the practice's reputation?
— Can the practice make a reasonable return out of the commission?
— Does the practice have the necessary resources to perform the commission, or can it perform them in part and sublet other parts to those who are better equipped?

Having decided that the commission is one that the practice wishes to pursue, the architect will need to ensure that they understand as fully as possible what is required in order to make a full and well-considered proposal for undertaking the work. The sort of matters they will need to consider include:

— Do they understand the client and their interest in the project?
— Do they have sufficient information about the site and its context?
— Are the client's objectives clear in terms of building use, size, build cost, programme, sustainability, other consultants, procurement and other aspirations?
— Is the scope of services required clear?
— What are the anticipated terms and conditions of the appointment?

If they do not have the answers to these questions they will ask – and if you are not able to answer they will give you guidance.

Calculating fees and cash flow

Fee scales have been ruled as uncompetitive for some time now, so the RIBA is no longer able to publish such information, even indicatively.

In assessing their financial offer to the client, the architect will aim to reflect the value they will bring to the project. In a competitive situation they will look to understand what the client is seeking – is it simply the cheapest fee or will other factors weigh equally, or more heavily? Architects' proposals will be structured to emphasise those aspects they believe will find greatest favour with the client.

Architects will calculate fees taking into account a range of considerations, including:

— The personnel likely to be engaged on the project and the projected time to be spent by them
— The cost to them of delivering the work and their target profit
— The services to be provided
— The proposed procurement method (that is, how the building contractor will be engaged)
— The proposed timescale for the project
— The added value they feel they can bring to the project.

Once estimated, the fee may be expressed in a number of different ways including:

— A percentage of the construction cost
— A lump sum for the entire project
— Calculated lump sums for each work stage (refer to Chapter 4 Project process for an explanation of the stages)
— Charges based on an hourly rate and a calculation of hours to be worked against these rates
— A combination of any of the above.

The fee proposal should set out a clear programme for the drawdown of fees throughout the life of the project. A monthly payment schedule establishes a regular invoicing routine for the benefit of both architect and client.

It is a requirement of both the ARB and RIBA codes of conduct that the architect ensures that they have adequate skills and resources to undertake the project which the client is proposing.

If the architect does not have sufficient resources to deliver the requirements of the project brief, they may consider subletting parts of the work to others with the necessary skills and resource. If this is the case, the architect is obliged to state clearly what services have been included in the fee proposal, together with a list of assumptions made and conditions of the offer.

The RIBA publishes standard forms of agreement which include schedules of design services and role specifications. The schedule of services describes typical services that may be performed depending on differing forms of procurement of the building work. (See Chapter 4 for further advice on appointing an architect and the standard forms available. See Chapter 6 for information on the standard form building contracts and for an explanation of the different options for building procurement.)

Areas of interface between different consultants need to be clearly defined and the architect may provide a matrix of services to be performed by each of the consultants, plus the client and contractor, with their offer.

There is a wide range of additional services the architect can be asked to provide including:

— Principal designer (under the CDM Regulations) (refer to Chapter 7: Construction (Design and Management) Regulations 2015 for an explanation of this important role)
— Interior designer
— Project manager
— Construction manager
— Party wall surveyor
— Planning consultant
— Surveyor.

All of the above require specialist knowledge and expertise and you should check that any architect, or a subconsultant appointed by them, has the necessary skills, experience and professional indemnity (PI) insurance cover to perform these services.

Refer to Chapter 5: Other consultants for an explanation of the work typically carried out by other construction professionals you may need to engage.

04

APPOINTING AN ARCHITECT – AGREEING THE TERMS AND THE SCOPE OF WORK

Private domestic homeowner

"

We were so pleased with the great experience and vision of [our] architects – we would do it again. **"**

Both the ARB and RIBA codes of professional conduct require architects to record the terms of their appointment before undertaking any work, and to have the necessary competence and resources. A written agreement is therefore essential: setting out what the architect will be doing, the timescale for the work and the fee and payment arrangements. The agreement should record the services to be provided, state the obligations of each party, identify the associated terms and conditions, and set out the fee basis and method of payment.

Individual architects are required to be registered with the ARB and are subject to its Code and to the disciplinary sanction of the ARB in relation to complaints of unacceptable professional conduct or serious professional incompetence.

As the client, you should write out what you hope to achieve through the project (the 'outcomes') and any specific briefing requirements, plus the total available budget and any key milestone dates (e.g. for determination of a planning application and/or for completion of the construction work).

The architect will use the information you provide to prepare a fee proposal and once this has been accepted the agreement can be written up. It is a requirement of the ARB and RIBA codes that the agreement is in writing.

For small projects, the agreement may be set out in a self-contained letter of appointment that outlines the obligations of both parties. The RIBA produces a book entitled *A Guide to Letter Contracts for Very Small Projects, Surveys and Reports*, which gives detailed guidance on such letter contracts, and includes model letters. (Further information on this publication is available at **www.ribabookshops.com**.)

However, it is recommended that you use a standard form such as the RIBA Domestic Professional Services Contract, also available at **www.ribabookshops.com**.

RIBA Domestic Professional Services Contract

The RIBA Domestic Professional Services Contract is between the 'customer' (the person or persons that wish to commission the professional services, known as the 'services') and the architect/consultant (the person or organisation performing the services). The contract is suitable for commissions for simple domestic projects of any value, in which the building works will be carried out using forms of building contract (ie with the contract with the builder), such as the RIBA Domestic Building Contract.

It is intended to be used as an agreement with a consumer relating to work to their home, including renovations, extensions, maintenance and new buildings, providing that the customer has decided to use the contract in their own name (i.e. not as a limited company or other legal entity or where the property will be let).

The RIBA Domestic Professional Services Contract is suitable for commissions procured on the basis of a traditional form of building contract where tendering occurs at the end of Stage 4 Technical Design. If the building contract is to be procured on other forms, such as design and build (D&B) or management types of contract, then the RIBA Standard or Concise Professional Services Contract would be more suitable, with adaption to suit a domestic/consumer building contract. (Refer to Chapter 6: Project process for explanations of the various stages of a project and options for procurement of the building.)

A contract with a consumer is subject to the Consumer Rights Act 2015 (see Chapter 8: Relevant legislation).

The contract terms should be compatible with the complexity of the project and the risks to each party and the terms of the agreement. The architect should explain and agree the Conditions of Appointment, the schedule of services and any appendices with you, the customer, as a 'consumer' (see below).

The RIBA Domestic Professional Services Contract is not suitable for works where the property is to be let or commercial or residential work undertaken for business clients including charities, religious organisations, not-for-profit bodies or where the customer is a public authority.

Negotiating the terms of a contract, for consumer customers

You are a 'consumer', so your architect is obliged to read through the terms of the agreement with you and individually explain each term in the context of your rights. Failure to do so could lead to certain terms of the agreement being invalidated.

This should enable you to 'influence the substance' of the terms. From the architect's point of view, this will minimise the risk that subsequently they would be considered to be unfair.

Some examples of terms that may be unfair under the Consumer Rights Act include:

— Fees and charges hidden in the small print
— Something that tries to limit your legal rights
— Disproportionate default charges
— Excessive early termination charges.

Ask your architect in particular to explain:

— Payment and payment notices
— The contractual limitation period and the limitation of liability in amount
— Professional indemnity (PI) insurance
— Net contribution clause
— Dispute resolution.

Your architect is obliged to record the substance of any discussions and any amendments that are agreed, so that it can be shown that the contract accords with the regulations.

If, as the client, you are a married couple or joint residential occupiers it is good practice to identify one of you as your representative with full authority to act on behalf of the other/s. This will save any confusion with regard to instructions given to the architect.

For work to your home or to a second home, you will be exempt from any statutory duties arising under the:

— Housing Grants, Construction and Regeneration Act 1996 as amended by Part 8 of the Local Democracy, Economic Development and Construction Act 2009, as a 'residential occupier' (see Chapter 8 Relevant legislation)
— Late Payment of Commercial Debts (Interest) Regulations 2002.

However, if your second home is to be let at any time as a holiday rental or to other tenants, you will be deemed to be a business client and the exemptions will not apply. In those circumstances, this contract is unsuitable and the RIBA Concise Professional Services Contract should be used instead. You should also refer to the sister publication to this book: *A Commercial Client's Guide to Engaging an Architect.*

Client's rights and obligations

As the client, you have various obligations under the contract. The main ones are:

— Advising the architect/consultant of the project requirements and of any subsequent changes required
— Providing the information which is necessary for the proper and timely performance of the services
— Giving decisions and approvals necessary for the performance of the services
— Paying the architect/consultant for the services performed
— Appointing or otherwise engaging other appointments required to perform work or services under separate agreements and requiring them to collaborate with the architect/consultant.

You also have rights under the contract. The most important is the right to suspend or terminate the architect/consultant's services.

Architect/consultant's rights and obligations

The architect/consultant has various obligations under the contract. The main ones are:

— Exercising reasonable skill, care and diligence in performing the services

— Performing the services with due regard to the client's brief

— Advising on progress in the performance of the services, of any information, decision or action required or of any issue that may materially affect the delivery, cost or quality of the project

— Collaborating with any other parties appointed or otherwise engaged by the client to perform work or services.

The architect/consultant also has rights under the contract. The most important are:

— The right to retain copyright in the drawings, data and documents produced in performing the services (the client is given a licence to copy and use the drawings, data and documents for purposes related to the construction of the project)

— The right to suspend or terminate performance of the services because of the client's failure to pay any fees or other amounts due.

Other standard forms

Other standard forms that may be considered for use can be found at **www.ribabookshops.com**. Your architect can advise you on this.

THE CONTEMPORARY LEAN-TO

ARCHITECT: **DOMA ARCHITECTS**

CLIENT: **CONFIDENTIAL**

COMPLETION: **2015**

The Contemporary Lean-to is the name given to work that Doma Architects designed to reconfigure the basement of a large Victorian semi-detached house in Harrogate, Yorkshire. The project has won numerous awards and was long-listed for the RIBA House of the Year 2016.

Pre-conversion, the living space was fragmented, with no real focus. The dark basement was cut off and used purely for storage. The rear garden could only be accessed down external stairs. The owner-clients had a job keeping an eye on their very young children. In short, the house had bags of potential that was choked off in an unsympathetic layout.

In 2013 the clients heard about the 'Architect in the House' charitable scheme. In return for a donation to Shelter, an architect would give them an initial free consultation. That's how they met Ruth Donnelly of Doma Architects and ended up appointing them: 'She was on the same wavelength as us. She had a really good fixed price introductory package which was very valuable since it was a step into the unknown for us.'

The clients eventually appointed Doma to provide full architectural services through to completion, and were very impressed: 'Ruth agreed a project plan with the contractor, and they pretty much finished on the day that they said they would. Her specification was very thorough, too, which made it clear what we were paying for.'

They were after something a little bit different, and were genuinely bowled over by the end result. The external stair was enfolded into the house under the eponymous lean-to, making a fascinating new connection to the basement, which is now the main living space. Access to the garden is through giant glass doors at the rear, which gives the house a new focus.

The many subtle architectural touches are critical to its success. 'You watch *Grand Designs* and think it all sounds a bit poncey and that it can't possibly make a difference. But it actually does.'

Overall, the relationship was extremely constructive: 'It's important to have people you trust. She listened to us and added an awful lot of her own ideas and experience, and proved to be reliable. We would definitely use them again.'

05

ENGAGING OTHER CONSULTANTS

Other than the architect, you may need to appoint other consultants Your architect can make recommendations or you can consult the relevant professional institutions.

Quantity surveyor/cost consultant

The role of the quantity surveyor (QS) or cost consultant is broadly related to the financial management of the project. The QS will be responsible for preparing a cost plan for the design and this should be kept up to date to reflect the current design proposal as the design evolves.

On smaller projects the architect may be able to undertake this service

It is critical that the cost of the design is managed proactively so that the design is not subsequently found to be unaffordable and subject to cost-cutting, or 'value engineering' as it is sometimes termed.

— **www.rics.org**

Structural engineer

The structural engineer advises on and prepares the structural design for the project, including the foundation design. They can advise the architect on local conditions relevant to the site, such as soil and geotechnical factors, roads, sewers, water supply and so on. They can identify hazards and hazardous substances, arrange for site, structural and drainage surveys, advise on alternative structural solutions, prepare design criteria and calculations, and advise on structural aspects of party walls, temporary structures and demolition work.

On domestic extensions the architect may be able to calculate the size of structural columns, beams, lintels and roof timbers.

— **www.istructe.org**

— **www.ice.org.uk**

Mechanical and electrical building services engineer

The mechanical and electrical (M&E) engineers will advise on and prepare designs for the various service systems in the building. They will advise on climatic conditions, energy use and conservation, emission problems and so on, and will consult relevant authorities as necessary. Increasingly, they play a role in delivering environmentally sustainable solutions and undertaking sustainable design audits. From this point of view it is important that they are involved early in the design process, when key decisions on sustainability have to be made.

On domestic projects the architect may be able to specify heating and plumbing or the contractor can do this as part of their contract.

— **www.imeche.org**

— **www.cibse.org**

Principal designer

Refer to Chapter 7 for information on this important role.

Planning consultant

On projects in sensitive locations, in conservation areas and with work to listed buildings it may be appropriate to appoint a specialist planning consultant. Your architect will be able to advise on this.

Interior designer

Many architects provide interior design services and see this as part of the offer, but you may wish to consider appointing a specialist interior designer for more unusual or bespoke interior design proposals.

Party wall surveyor

Refer to Chapter 8.

Landscape architect

Where the project has an extensive landscaped element, it may be appropriate to appoint a landscape architect either directly or through the architect as a subconsultant. Your architect will be able to advise you on this.

Surveyor

If a measured survey of an existing property is required, you will either need to appoint a surveyor or the architect may be able to undertake the work. For larger projects this is likely to be a specialist service. Your architect will be able to advise on this. It is likely that the survey will be required before design activities can commence.

Construction manager

A construction manager (CM) will manage the subcontractors in construction management contract, including organising the tender and administering their contracts. Critically, the CM is responsible for coordinating the interfaces between the subcontractors. This role can be undertaken by the client, or the architect may be able to perform the role.

06 PROJECT PROCESS – KEY STAGES IN DEVELOPING THE BUILDING

"

As we live in a conservation area we wanted to extend our Victorian cottage but didn't want to add something that bore no relation to the original building. Our architect had experience of similar projects and devised a sensitive scheme which, on the inside, gives us the additional rooms we need but on the outside stays true to the character of the house. By using traditional materials and focusing on the details we've created something we can be really proud of. "

All projects go through more or less the same process: from the initial briefing; through development of the design; applying for planning permission where this is required; producing the technical drawings for Building Regulations and for construction purposes; tendering; and finally construction plus, where required, post-construction activities. In some circumstances tendering is carried out at an earlier stage and this is explained below.

The first thing an architect will do is ask questions, listen and understand what you are trying to achieve. They will work with you to develop your project brief and finalise the budget. It is essential that you agree these with your architect before starting the project.

A good architect will develop solutions and propose ways to reduce costs while coming up with a design that will increase the building's value. They will guide you through a whole range of processes – from coming up with an initial design to seeing the project through planning and construction to completion.

The RIBA has developed a 'Plan of Work' which sets out these stages to a standard that is used by the whole UK construction industry. It was initially developed in 1963, but the latest version was published in 2013 with some fundamental changes.

A version of the Plan of Work 2013 specifically designed for small projects is set out on pages 30–31. Further information on the Plan of Work can be found at **www.ribaplanofwork.com**.

It has eight stages, numbered 0–7. The Plan notes activities that need to take place at each stage and these are set out below the stage headings. It is important to note that planning permission is not a stage but rather an activity that usually takes place during Stage 3.

You can commission an architect for any of the stages you need for your project, but it is recommended that they are engaged through Stages 1–6. On smaller projects some clients will engage the architect only up to receipt of planning permission (typically Stage 3). This should be done with caution because you will be tendering with little information and this can lead to reduced quality and poor cost control during construction. An alternative strategy is to appoint the architect to make the Building Regulations application (after receipt of planning approval) and use the associated drawings, schedules and specifications for tendering. However the most satisfactory method is to procure a full set of tender information. Also remember that you will be acting as the construction contract administrator, which can be a demanding role. For further information on this refer to Stages 4–6 below.

The RIBA Plan of Work 2013

Stage 0 – Strategic Definition

Stage 0 is the period of consideration of the requirements or needs that may (but may not) lead to a construction project. This is usually prior to engagement of any professional advice, although on large projects it may be appropriate to recruit the services of a RIBA Client Adviser. See Chapter 13: Client Advisers.

Stage 0 is where you, as the client, decide there may be a need for construction and consider the desired outcomes. It may be that they can be met without recourse to a building project, but where the case is clear, or where further consideration is required to determine the need, an architect should be engaged to undertake feasibility studies which take place in Stage 1.

It is during Stage 0 that you consider which architect to appoint, as well as other consultants where required. The architect can advise on the need for other consultants during Stage 1 if this is needed.

Refer to Chapter 2: Selecting an architect and Chapter 4: Appointing an architect, for further advice on selecting and appointing an architect.

It is important to write down the outcomes you want to achieve (the Strategic Brief) and issue these to the architect/s at the start of the engagement process. The brief may develop or even change later on, but your initial thoughts are a critical starting point.

Under the RIBA Plan of Work the briefing process is set out in three parts: Stage 0 – Strategic Brief; Stage 1 – Initial Project Brief; Stage 2 – Final Project Brief. This is in recognition that the brief evolves and develops during the initial design phases.

The ultimate success of your project depends on the quality of your brief; that is, your ability to describe to your architect clearly the requirements and functions of your building and the proposed methods of operation and management. It is wise to ask your architect to assist you in preparing the next stage of the brief (termed the Initial Project Brief).

Your architect will need to know:

— Your aims – what outcomes you want to achieve
— Your reasons for embarking on the building project and what activities are intended for it
— Your budget (remember this needs to allow for fees, disbursements and VAT, as well as the actual cost of the building works)
— Who will be making the decisions about the designs, costs and day-to-day matters when the project is underway
— Your interest in environmentally sustainable design.

Stage 1 – Preparation and Brief

This is the most important part of the project and is where the architect can add the most value. The architect will assist you in developing your

Strategic Brief into the Initial Project Brief and will undertake some preliminary appraisals to assess the options and feasibility of the project This can range from a sketch design solution to a full feasibility study and will enable you to decide on the best way forward. They will identify the need for any approvals and other consultants, most commonly a structural engineer. Chapter 5 notes other consultants you may need to engage.

At the initial meetings, your architect will listen carefully to your intention and help develop the brief alongside the design. Timings and budgets for your project will be defined at an early stage and only after you have approved initial sketches will the ideas be developed further.

The RIBA has developed a Briefing and Evaluation Toolkit that can be employed. Your architect will be able to advise you on its use.

Stage 2 – Concept Design

The architect will develop the Initial Project Brief into a Final Project Brief, alongside the concept design. The architect may present a number of concepts for you to choose from. They will also liaise with the local planning authority. The Final Project Brief should be completed by the end of Stage 2 and should reflect your detailed requirements and aspirations. Once it has been completed it should be considered fixed and any changes to it during Stage 3 onwards should go through 'change process' whereby any financial, programme and quality matters are considered before proceeding with the change. In this way, you will have better control over these three criteria which are considered to be the cornerstone measures of all building projects.

Stage 3 – Developed Design

During this stage the conceptual ideas are developed, with the other consultants as required, into a coordinated design. Once you have approved the design proposals your architect will submit them for planning approval, if required. This usually occurs during Stage 3 but can be submitted during Stage 2. Bringing the planning application forward can have risks and the architect will be able to explain the relative merits of submitting the application at different stages in the design process.

Stage 4 – Technical Design

During this stage the architect, and any other consultants, will prepare the technical drawings and specification/s and/or a schedule of work that will be used for tendering and for construction of the building. The architect can invite and appraise tenders from building contractors. Tendering can take place earlier in the design process. There are broadly three methods of procuring buildings:

1. Traditional
2. Design and build
3. Construction management.

Your architect will be able to advise on the most appropriate form of procurement, but a brief description of each is given in the box (below).

The three options for building procurement

Traditional

In traditional procurement, the design is fully detailed before seeking tenders. In this way, the contractor is pricing a full set of information, and cost and quality can be controlled. However, it comes at the price of taking longer overall. The quality depends on having a comprehensive set of technical drawings and specifications at tender stage. This is the form of procurement used on most domestic projects.

Design and build

In D&B, the contractor prices the job at an earlier stage and usually before a full set of technical drawings has been produced. The contractor will then be responsible for developing the final technical design. The contractor also fixes their price, and so this form of procurement brings programme benefits and cost certainty, but it can be at the expense of quality because the details and specification may be reduced (while still technically complying with the tender information). This is appropriate for straightforward projects but is not normally used for domestic buildings, because it tends only to be used on larger, commercial projects.

Construction management

In managed procurement, a consultant or the client themselves acts as main contractor but subcontracts the various 'trades' (e.g. foundations, external walls, roof, plumbing). This form of procurement has time and, potentially, quality benefits, but needs skilled leadership to manage the interfaces between the 'packages' and to control cost. It is typical for self-build projects but it can be difficult to control the overall cost of the project.

It is broadly accepted that of the three measures of project success – quality, cost and programme – any one form of procurement will deliver two of these but not all three in equal measure. So 'traditional' forms of procurement will deliver better quality and cost control but will take longer; D&B will bring cost and programme certainty but at the expense of quality; and 'managed' forms of procurement will bring quality and programme benefits but will bring less certainty of cost control.

Choice of procurement route is an important consideration that will have a significant effect on the outcome of your project, and your architect will be able to advise on the best solution for your particular situation.

It is recommended that the RIBA Domestic Building Contract is used for the contract with the builder. This can be purchased from **www.ribabookshops.com**. The contract is written in plain English and has advantages over and greater flexibility than the other contracts available. Your architect will be able to advise you on this.

Stage 5 – Construction

With the (usual) traditional form of procurement, throughout the construction phase the architect can administer your contract with the builder, carry out regular inspections, deal with queries, instruct any additional work required, monitor progress on site, keep track of cost and certify payments due to the builder.

It is important to understand that the contract with the builder/contractor is between you – the client – and the builder. The architect can administer the contract on your behalf but is not actually a party to it. The architect will be able to explain this important distinction to you in more detail.

When the project is ready to hand over, the architect – if they have been appointed as contract administrator – will inspect the building and issue a certificate of Practical Completion once the works have been finished in accordance with the contract documents. This is the final activity in Stage 5.

Insurance

It is very important that you have the necessary insurance cover to any existing building before construction work begins. Speak to your buildings insurance provider and tell them what work is being undertaken and the anticipated duration. Remember to notify the insurer when the work has been completed.

Make sure also that the contractor takes out insurance to cover the works and against injury to third parties. This should include:

— Public liability insurance to cover injury to a third party (such as a passing pedestrian) and damage to third-party property
— Employer's liability insurance, which is a legal requirement for limited companies and covers injury to employees
— Contractors' all-risk cover (which many builders do not bother with), which covers accidental damage to work carried out by the builder before completion or before the homeowner's policy has been extended to cover it.

Note that if the contractor is undertaking design activities they should also have professional indemnity (PI) insurance.

Stage 6 – Handover and Close Out

The architect will be available after completion to assist in the handover process. If they are the contract administrator, they will also certify the final payment, usually six or 12 months after Practical Completion following the defects fixing period. This is a period allowed for any defects or shrinkages to be picked up, following which the contractor will return to site to make good. A small amount of the contract sum is held back ('retention') until this has been carried out.

Stage 7 – In Use

Stage 7 is the building in use and is not generally a stage where there is specific work undertaken by the architect. The exception is where some form of post-occupancy evaluation is undertaken, for example to assess the energy efficiency of the building. This sort of exercise is more typical of larger developments for clients where lessons can be learned for future developments. If such exercises are to be undertaken, they would usually be under a separate appointment.

RIBA
Plan of Work

Small Project Plan of Work

The RIBA Plan of Work organises the process of briefing, designing, constructing, maintaining, operating and using building projects into 8 stages.

The RIBA Small Project Plan of Work has been published to enable closer working between clients and architects and to suggest the key tasks for small projects. It should be used in conjunction with the RIBA Plan of Work 2013 to organise project tasks, as many tasks are left out of this document to keep it as simple as possible.

The **Sustainability Checkpoints**, that provide sustainable design tasks relevant at all project scales, and further information on **Project Strategies** can be found at www.ribaplanofwork.com.

The RIBA Plan of Work 2013 should be used solely as guidance for the preparation of detailed professional services contracts and building contracts.

Stages	**0** Strategic Definition	**1** Preparation and Brief	**2** Concept Design
Tasks			
Core Objectives	Identify client's **Business Case** and **Strategic Brief** and other core project requirements.	Develop **Project Objectives**, **Project Outcomes**, **Sustainability Aspirations**, **Project Budget**, other parameters or constraints and develop **Initial Project Brief**. Undertake **Feasibility Studies** and review of **Site Information**.	Prepare Concept Design including outline propos for structural design, building services system outline specifications an preliminary **Cost Inform** along with relevant **Proje Strategies** in accordanc **Design Programme**. Agree alterations to brie issue **Final Project Brief.**
	[Sustainability Checkpoint – 0]	[Sustainability Checkpoint – 1]	[Sustainability Checkpoin
Procurement Professional services and building contracts based on a traditional procurement route	Initial considerations for assembling the project team.	Agree **Schedule of Services**. Appoint design team including **Principal Designer**.	
Planning Consent, Building Regulations and Health and Safety (CDM) Overview of regulatory requirements.		Conduct initial pre-**Planning** application discussions, [if required to determine the suitability of **Feasibility Studies**]. inform **Client** of their regulatory responsibilities including **Health and Safety**.	Collate **Pre-Constructic Information.** Conduct pre-**Planning** application discussions Submit outline planning applications. [Detailed planning applications should be only where to meet spe client need, the associa risks should be include Stage sign-off].
Information Exchanges Generally at stage completion	**Strategic Brief.**	**Initial Project Brief.**	Concept Design includi outline structural and b services design, prelimi **Cost Information** and **P Project Brief.**
Level of Detail Suggested level of detail for design and level of information for specification [If using BIM the model will be a deliverable.]			1:1250 Location Plan. 1:500 Site Plan. 1:100 Plans, Sections a Elevations.

© RIBA 2016

...eloped ...ign	4 Technical Design	5 Construction	6 Handover and Closeout	7 In Use
...e Developed Design, ...ng coordinated ...dated proposals ...ctural design, ...g services systems, ...specifications, **Cost ...ation** and **Project ...es** in accordance with ...**Programme**.	Prepare Technical Design in accordance with **Project Strategies** to include all architectural, structural and building services information, specialist subcontractor design and specifications, in accordance with **Design Programme**.	Offsite manufacturing and onsite Construction in accordance with the **Construction Programme** and resolution of **Design Queries** from site as they arise.	Handover of building and conclusion of **Building Contract**.	Undertake In Use services in accordance with **Schedule of Services**.
...ability Checkpoint – 3]	[Sustainability Checkpoint – 4]	[Sustainability Checkpoint – 5]	[Sustainability Checkpoint – 6]	[Sustainability Checkpoint – 7]
	Issue **Technical Design** for tender. Tenders assessed and **Building Contract** awarded including appointing **Principal Contractor**. Specialist sub-contractor Stage 4 information reviewed post award.	Administer **Building Contract** to **Practical Completion**, including regular site inspections and review of progress.	Conclude administration of **Building Contract**.	Maintain relationship with Client, offer additional In Use services as appointed.
Planning application. ...ake third party ...ations as required. ...d planning ...tions should only be ...rior to the design ...ation activities if ...ed by the client. The ...coordination activities ...be concluded prior to ...completion].	Review **Planning Conditions** following granting of consent. Discharge pre-Construction **Planning Conditions** as required and others where possible. Prepare and submit **Building Regulations** submission and any other third party submissions requiring consent.	Collate **Health and Safety File**. **Contractor** to comply with any construction-specific **Planning Conditions**.	Comply with pre-occupancy **Planning Conditions**. Advise **Client** of need to comply with in-use **Planning Conditions**.	
...ed Design, including ...rdinated architectural, ...al and building ...design and updated ...ormation.	Completed Technical Design of the project.		**'As-constructed' Information** including **Health and Safety File** [at beginning of stage] **Feedback** reports.	
...ocation Plan. ...te Plan. ...ans, Sections and ...ns. ...etch Details. ...**Specification**.	1:500 Block Plan. 1:100 Site plan including drainage, external works, etc. 1:50 Plans, Sections and Elevations. 1:20 Detailed plans and sections. 1:10/1:5/Full Size component details Door/Window/Finishes and other Schedules. Detailed **Specification**.		1:100 Site plan including drainage, external works, etc. 1:50 Plans, Sections and Elevations. Detailed Specification. Structural, building services and specialist subcontractor information [as appropriate if not incorporated onto the architects information].	

07

CONSTRUCTION (DESIGN AND MANAGEMENT) REGULATIONS 2015

The Construction (Design and Management) Regulations 2015 (abbreviated to the CDM Regulations) are the regulations for managing the health, safety and welfare of construction projects. It is a tragic statistic that, on average, there is close to one death per week on UK construction sites and many serious, life-changing injuries. The CDM Regulations aim to prevent such incidents through consideration of potential hazards in the design and construction process. The Regulations impose duties on the client, the principal designer and other designers, and the principal contractor and other contractors.

As domestic clients are not considered likely to have the necessary skills knowledge and experience, their duties are normally transferred to:

— The contractor, on a single contractor project, or;
— The principal contractor, on a project involving more than one contractor.

Under the Regulations, domestic clients are defined as people who have construction work carried out on their own home, or the home of a family member, that is not done in furtherance of a business, whether for profit or not.

Where a domestic client has appointed an architect or other designer they can, by written agreement, transfer the client duties to the architect designer. Where no such agreement is made, the principal contractor automatically takes on the client's responsibilities. If a domestic client fails to make the appointments required, the designer in control of the preconstruction phase of the project is the principal designer and the contractor in control of the construction phase of the project the principal contractor.

The client duties that are transferred relate to such matters as making suitable arrangements for managing the project, including making su that the principal designer and principal contractor are appointed and that sufficient time and resources are allocated to the project. They also relate to making sure that relevant information is prepared and provided to other duty holders; that the principal designer and principal contractor carry out their duties; and that welfare facilities are provided.

08 RELEVANT LEGISLATION

Building Act 1984 and Building Regulations 2010

The Act and the Regulations apply to England and Wales and aim to secure standards regarding: health and safety for people in and around buildings; energy conservation; and the welfare and convenience of disabled people.

The Regulations apply to all new building work such as might be undertaken by domestic clients and impose duties covering design and construction of buildings, their services, fittings and equipment.

'Approved documents' set out the requirements and give practical and technical guidance on compliance with the Regulations. The approved documents are lettered A–R, and cover: structure, fire safety, site preparation, contaminants and resistance to moisture, toxic substances, sound transmission, ventilation, hygiene, drainage and waste disposal, heating appliances, protection from falling, conservation of fuel and power, access and facilities for disabled people, glazing, and electrical safety.

The local authority must be given notice before work commences. Building control inspectors will make independent checks on compliance and issue a final certificate on satisfactory completion.

There are two ways compliance with the Regulations is ensured – through local authority building control inspectors or approved inspector – either of which the client is free to use. Approved inspectors are private sector companies or individuals authorised to provide a building control service. Your architect will be able to explain this in more detail, as well as the alternative means of notification: a 'Building Notice' or a 'Full Plans' application.

CDM Regulations 2015

See Chapter 7.

Consumer Rights Act 2015

A contract with a consumer is subject to the Consumer Rights Act 2015. The Act requires that in all contracts for services:

— The trader must perform the service with reasonable care and skill
— The information which is said or written is binding where the consumer relies on it
— Where the price is not agreed beforehand the service must be provided for a reasonable price
— The service must be carried out in a reasonable time.

Refer to Chapter 4: Appointing an architect.

Know your rights

The Unfair Terms in Consumer Contracts Regulations 1999

The object of this legislation is to offer the consumer protection where the contracting parties might be of unequal bargaining strength and the terms of the contract have been drafted unilaterally.

You will be a 'consumer' if you sign a contract in your own name, not as a limited company or other legal entity. Legally, a consumer is described as 'a natural person acting for purposes outside their trade, business or profession'.

For work to your home or to a second home you will be exempt from the provisions of the Housing Grants, Construction and Regeneration Act 1996 as a 'residential occupier' and the Late Payment of Commercial Debts Regulations 2013.

If your second home is to be let at any time as a holiday rental or to other tenants these exemptions do not apply.

The terms of the RIBA Domestic Professional Services Contract recognise the importance of your consumer rights.

Equality Act 2010

The Act replaced previous anti-discrimination laws with a single Act to make the law simpler and to remove inconsistencies. This makes the law easier for people to understand and comply with. The Act also strengthened protection in some situations and covers nine protected characteristics that cannot be used as a reason to treat people unfairly Every person has one or more of the protected characteristics, so the Act protects everyone against unfair treatment. The protected characteristics are: age, disability, gender reassignment, marriage and civil partnership, pregnancy and maternity, race and religion or belief sex and sexual orientation.

The Equality Act sets out the different ways in which it is unlawful to treat someone, such as direct and indirect discrimination, harassment victimisation, and failing to make a reasonable adjustment for a disabled person.

The Act prohibits unfair treatment in the workplace, when providing goods, facilities and services, when exercising public functions and when buying or renting property.

European Services Directive

A key part of the European Services Directive relates to improving consumer confidence when conducting business anywhere in the European Union. It achieves this by setting some basic requirement – ensuring that customers have access to a minimum amount of information and to a complaints procedure. Certain information must be made available, including:

— The name, legal status and form, and address of the business
— If registered in a trade of other similar public register, the register' name and the registration number
— If carrying on a regulated profession, any professional body of similar institution with which the business is registered, the professional title and the country in which that title was granted
— If required to hold professional liability insurance or a guarantee information about the cover and contact details of the insurer an territorial coverage.

Housing Grants, Construction and Regeneration Act 1996

This Act applies to most construction contracts that include client-architect professional services agreements. However, the Act does not apply to a contract with a 'residential occupier' that principally relates to operations on a dwelling which one of the parties to the contract occupies or intends to occupy as their residence.

It is important to note that a construction contract need not be in writing for the Act to apply and a dispute arising from an oral contract can be referred to adjudication.

RIBA building contracts include terms to comply with the Act's provisions, which primarily relate to payment procedures and resolution of disputes by adjudication.

Party Wall etc. Act 1996

A notice must be served by or on behalf of the building owner notifying the owner and occupiers of adjoining land if:

— A party wall is to be demolished, rebuilt, extended or repaired
— A new building is to be constructed near the boundary
— A new party fence is to be built
— A new wall is to be built up to the boundary line.

If the adjoining owner does not consent to the works a dispute will arise. The Act sets out a procedure for resolving such disputes.

A party wall is one that either stands astride the boundary of land belonging to two (or more) different owners, or stands wholly on one owner's land but is used by two (or more) owners to separate their buildings. There are specific requirements that owners of such walls must meet when alterations are to be made.

For an explanation of party wall conditions and useful standard letters that can be used to manage the regulations pertaining to party walls, download the government guidance from **www.gov.uk/party-wall-etc-act-1996-guidance**.

Your architect may be able to provide advice on party walls, but you may also need to appoint a party wall surveyor. If you are not sure whether the Party Wall etc. Act applies to the work that you are planning you should seek professional advice from an organisation such as the Pyramus & Thisbe Club, whose website is **www.partywalls.org.uk** The club is a not-for-profit body of professionals that can put you in contact with local members who are willing to provide general and informal advice about the Act, and can usually provide you with names of party wall surveyors in your area.

Town and Country Planning Act 1990

The purpose of the planning system is to regulate the use, siting and appearance of buildings, and to protect the environment and public amenity.

All developments require planning permission from the local planning authority except for internal changes to your home (other than for listed properties) and certain small domestic extensions within strict criteria which may be covered by 'permitted development'. Internal or external alterations that would affect the character of a listed building of historical or architectural interest require two separate applications, one for listed building consent and one for planning permission. If the site is within a conservation area you will need conservation area consent as well.

THE LAKE DISTRICT
LOVE SHACK

ARCHITECT: **SUTHERLAND HUSSEY HARRIS ARCHITECTS**
CLIENT: **ADAM SUTHERLAND AND KAREN GUTHRIE**
COMPLETION: **2009**

The Lake District Love Shack these days is an extremely successful holiday let close to Lake Windermere. However, it started life as a home for its client-owners Karen Guthrie and Adam Sutherland, who is also Charlie Sutherland's (of Sutherland Hussey Harris Architects) half-brother.

Having bought the secluded woodland site in 2003, they replaced the existing chalet with an unapologetically contemporary bijou shack for two. The local planning authority now holds it up as a shining example of sensitive development despite its initial entrenched opposition to the scheme.

The clients had two main ambitions. First, they wanted a comfortable, sustainable home to live in for a year or so before selling it on. Second, they wanted to demonstrate that you could build a highly insulated modern home sympathetic to its natural setting. Given the region's comparatively long winters and short days, they were especially keen to avoid the vernacular slate-roofed, small-windowed house type that excludes daylight.

Armed with a small budget, they approached the RIBA to ask for details of local architects. In the end, though, they were able to entice Edinburgh-based Sutherland Hussey Harris to come on board. Mostly because of the family connection but also because the practice had another job on nearby, the relationship worked out well, with no arguments. Adam Sutherland remembers it fondly: 'The fun bit was the first stage when the architect is responding to the brief with different solutions and doing sketch plans.'

That's not to say that the project was trouble free. Securing planning permission was lengthy, confrontational and unexpectedly expensive. However, guided by Sutherland Hussey Harris, they finally won consent in 2007. Building began in 2008, completing in 2009 with successful results. As Adam Sutherland says: 'Living in a home with so much daylight is a revelation. The contrast to the hideously ugly home we had been living in was spectacular.'

Adam Sutherland is unusually thoughtful about how clients can get the best out of their architect. He thinks of them as a creative force. 'The tragedy is that most people use them as glorified builders. It's important not to lose their creative potential.'

The clients decided not to sell in the end but instead set it up as holiday let. Bucking the trend, the Love Shack books up all year round, even in winter.

09

RIBA
CHARTERED PRACTICES

Only architectural practices that meet strict eligibility criteria can registe
as a RIBA Chartered Practice. They comply with strict criteria covering
insurance, health and safety and quality management systems. They
range from one-person offices to large, multinational firms operating
worldwide. RIBA Chartered Practices are the only architectural practices
endorsed and promoted by the RIBA. The requirements for RIBA
Chartered Practice membership are as follows:

— At least one of the practice's full-time principals (director or partner
   must be a RIBA Chartered Member and on the ARB register
— All of the practice's architectural work must be supervised by a
   RIBA Chartered Member who is on the ARB register
— At least one in eight of all staff employed in the practice must be
   on the ARB register, or an Associate Member of the RIBA or a CIA
   member with RIBA Affiliate Membership
— At least one in 10 of all staff employed in the practice must be a
   RIBA Chartered Member or Associate Member
— The practice must have a current and appropriate professiona
   indemnity (PI) insurance policy
— The practice must operate an appropriate quality managemen
   system
— The practice must operate an appropriate health and safety polic
— The practice must have a written employment policy in place whic
   addresses the principles of the RIBA policy statement on employmen
— The practice must have an appropriate equality, diversity an
   inclusion policy in place
— The practice must have an appropriate continuing professiona
   development (CPD) framework in place
— The practice must operate an appropriate environmenta
   management policy
— The practice must commit to paying at least the Living Wag
   (or London Living Wage, where appropriate) to architecture student
   working within the practice.

All practices registered with the RIBA Chartered Practice scheme and their staff are expected to conduct themselves in accordance with a code of practice and in a manner appropriate to their Chartered Practice status, and the practice will be liable to reprimand, suspension or expulsion if they do not.

The *Code of Practice for RIBA Chartered Practices* comprises three principles of professional conduct and practice – honesty/integrity, competence, and relationships – and the professional values that support those principles. A copy of the Code can be downloaded by searching 'RIBA chartered practice code' at **www.architecture.com**.

10 ARB AND RIBA CODES OF CONDUCT

All qualified architects must maintain membership of the Architect's Registration Board (ARB). Architects are expected to:

1. Be honest and act with integrity
2. Be competent
3. Promote your services honestly and responsibly
4. Manage your business competently
5. Consider the wider impact of your work
6. Carry out your work faithfully and conscientiously
7. Be trustworthy and look after your clients' money properly
8. Have appropriate insurance arrangements
9. Maintain the reputation of architects
10. Deal with disputes or complaints appropriately
11. Cooperate with regulatory requirements and Investigations
12. Have respect for others.

A copy of the ARB *Architects Code: Standards of Conduct and Practic* can be downloaded at **www.arb.org**

Architects who are members of the RIBA must abide by the RIBA Cod of Conduct. The purpose of this Code is to promote professional goo conduct and best practice. Members should at all times be guided b its spirit as well as its precise and express terms. Any member wh contravenes the Code will be liable to reprimand, suspension expulsion. Chartered Practices must abide by the Code of Practice Individual Members must abide by the Code of Professional Conduc Both Codes have identical principles – Integrity, Competence an Relationships.

Members must comply with all relevant legal obligations. It is not th remit of the Code to duplicate the provisions of business, employmen health and safety, environmental and discrimination law.

Members' conduct outside the practice of architecture will not normally fall within the remit of the Code and the institute's disciplinary procedures, unless the disciplinary committee determines that such conduct generally offends against the honour and integrity of the profession.

A judgment from a competent court or tribunal against a member in their professional capacity as an architect may be considered sufficient evidence of a breach of the Code.

Copies of the Code can be downloaded by searching 'RIBA Code of Conduct' at **www.architecture.com**.

11

RIBA FIND AN ARCHITECT

Dharmacharini
Maitrivajri, London
Buddhist Centre

"

I am indebted to the architects for many things; their whole-heartedness for one. Each stage of the process has been characterised by their determination to do the best job possible and their commitment to a high level of architectural detail. The creativity and skill of the design team meant our imaginations of what was possible grew. "

The RIBA's online directory can help clients create a shortlist from ove 3,000 RIBA Chartered Practices and 40,000 projects. Go to:

— **www.architecture.com**

Alternatively, the RIBA Client Services team will create a shortlist c Chartered Practices with the right skills and experience on your beha They only suggest accredited Chartered Practices, who meet the RIBA standards of quality and service.

The service is confidential and provided free of charge.

The RIBA Client Services team can be reached at 020 7307 3700 c email **clientservices@riba.org**.

12

RIBA COMPETITIONS

Private domestic homeowner

"

We approached our architects to design an individual extension to a very small, 19th century Manx Cottage, which would allow us 21st century living without losing the charm of the setting, which includes views over the Manx hills and out to the Irish Sea. Their inspiration to hide the extension into the hillside whilst providing panoramic views was bold and imaginative. Giving as much information to your architect about your background, values and vision goes a long way to seeing these important ideas translated into your new home. Our architects were very receptive to our ideas and interests. "

RIBA Competitions has extensive experience of delivering high-profile selection processes. Established for over 40 years, they manage competitions for a diverse range of project types and budgets on behalf of both public and private sector clients. They are widely recognised as the UK's leading provider of design competition management services, and can advise and arrange competitive selection processes to meet client's requirements. Using the RIBA to manage and support a competition brings credibility, prestige and rigour to the process.

With the RIBA brand you are sending a very clear signal to contestants that your competition will be efficient and fair, and that it will adhere to best practice standards. The RIBA can use multiple routes to promote your competition, including direct to its 40,000+ global membership.

Fees and a timetable are agreed with you at the outset so there are no hidden extras along the way.

For further information call 0113 203 1490, email **riba.competitions@riba.org** or go to **www.architecture.com**

What is a design competition?

Within the built environment, 'design competition' is the collective term for any process inviting architects and other related design professionals to compete against each other for a commission or prize.

The majority of competitions involve the submission and evaluation of project-specific design proposals. For publicly-funded projects, competitions must be organised to comply with public procurement legislation, if the value of the project or subsequent commission is likely to exceed specified thresholds. Whether or not competitions are subject to public procurement legislation, there is still a need for a fair, properly scrutinised, well-managed process.

RIBA competitions are generally only used for larger projects, but there is no hard and fast rule. A minimum might be considered £500,000 construction value, although above £1 million is more typical. The decision to run a competition for smaller value projects really depends on the nature of the project, what the client is looking to achieve and whether the cost of organising the process represents value for money for them.

Why run a design competition?

The appointment of a design professional is the single most important task when undertaking a project in the built environment. Finding a suitable designer, even for a small private project, becomes a priority from an early stage. There are a number of ways of selecting a designer such as personal recommendation, previous experience, research or existing framework. However, a competition based on evaluating the relative merits of several designers can give a client the best opportunity to make an informed selection. The competition system is the only recognised formal process which provides these specific benefits. A design competition offers many advantages, but may not always be appropriate (e.g. where a client already has a team with whom they have a trusted, established working relationship). However, a design competition can be a highly successful procurement model because it can help prioritise good design and bring the highest quality of thinking to a project. Competitions have a reputation for giving the best range of design options to choose from at a fraction of the total construction cost of a scheme. A competition can be used to select a design team including developers, a construction consortium or a design solution.

If you are unsure if a competition is right for your project then it is worth seeking further advice from RIBA Competitions. Mentoring advice is also available from previous clients on request.

13 | RIBA CLIENT ADVISERS

If you are undertaking a large or complex project the RIBA can put you in touch with an accredited RIBA Client Adviser, an experienced architect who can help define and prepare the brief, set up and lead the project team, draw up the business case and manage the procurement on your behalf.

However you structure your decision-making process, make sure that one person is designated as the point of contact between you and the architect.

If you are thinking about appointing an RIBA Client Adviser you can contact RIBA Client Services on 020 7307 3700 or email **clientservices@riba.org**. For further advice go to **www.architecture.com/working-with-an-architect/client-adviser**

14 MANAGING DISPUTES

Building projects are complicated, and despite the numerous checks and balances of the procedures and codes set out in this book, a dispute between the parties can sometimes arise. When this happens you need to have recourse to a means of managing the situation that minimises the impact on the project and the cost, and provides an appropriate resolution.

The RIBA Domestic Professional Services Contract (between you and the architect) and the RIBA Domestic Building Contract (between you and the builder) provide mechanisms for this through mediation and adjudication.

It is helpful to know what the most typical reasons for disputes are and to ensure, as far as possible, that they don't arise in the first place.

The best means of avoiding disputes is to have open and clear dialogue: first in communicating the brief; then in having a written contract as well as written instructions to confirm any changes made during the course of the project, because these usually carry cost.

Common issues include 'what does the fee cover' and 'what stage has the project reached'. The RIBA Plan of Work can be used to clarify what stage the project is at and as a framework for the scope of work to be covered with regard to the services to be provided by the architect and other professionals.

The contract is key to managing the client-architect and client-builder relationship. The contract should set out the duties, responsibilities and scope of work in sufficient detail that there can be no misunderstanding about what is and is not to be done by each party. When filled in properly, the RIBA forms provide this detail.

The contract must set out clearly the basis of the fee and what is extra.

RIBA and ARB codes of conduct regarding complaints

Article 3.5 of the RIBA Code of Professional Conduct states that:

'Members are expected to have in place (or have access to) effective procedures for dealing promptly and appropriately with disputes or complaints.'

The RIBA Code of Professional Conduct Guidance Note 8 notes:

'Members are expected to have a written procedure which handles disputes and complaints promptly... The complaints procedure must be available on request to any complainant' (client or other stakeholder).

Ensures that clients are informed of whom to approach in the event of a problem with the professional service provided; and handles disputes and complaints promptly.

Standard 10.1 and 10.2 of the ARB Architects Code states:

10.1 [The architect is] expected to have a written procedure for the handling of complaints which will be in accordance with the Code and published guidance.

10.2 Complaints should be handled courteously and promptly at every stage, and as far as practicable in accordance with the following time scales:

a) an acknowledgment within 10 working days from the receipt of a complaint; and

b) a response addressing the issues raised in the initial letter of complaint within 30 working days from its receipt.

10.3 If appropriate, [the architect] should encourage alternative methods of dispute resolution, such as mediation or conciliation.

RIBA Chartered Practices

Where the architect is a RIBA Chartered Practice they must abide by the Code of Practice for Chartered Practices. Clients can make a complaint if a Chartered Practice, or a member of their staff, is in breach of the Code. The RIBA publishes guidance on this which can be downloaded from **www.architecture.com**.

15

CLIENT CHECKLIST OF ACTIONS WITH KEY MILESTONES AND WATCH POINTS

The following is set out under the RIBA Plan of Work project stages. For an explanation of these see Chapter 6: Project process.

Stage 0	Strategic Definition	Completed
	Prepare Strategic Project Brief. (Refer to Chapter 6).	
	Consider project programme and budget.	
	Arrange any funding required.	
	Consider any project risks and make a note of them to pass on to the architect once appointed.	
	Agree a single point of contact to represent you as client to the project team, ie the architect, other consultants and, in due course, the contractor.	
	Review your client responsibilities under the CDM Regulations 2015. (Refer to Chapter 7).	
	Consider your position with regard to environmental sustainability and set this out in the brief.	
	Consider selection process and form of appointment to be used for contracting professional services. (Refer to Chapter 4).	
	Select and appoint architect/lead designer. (Refer to Chapter 4).	
	Select and appoint principal designer (under CDM Regulations), if appropriate. (Refer to Chapter 7). Note this is likely to be the architect/lead designer.	

	Collate any information you have on the existing site and building and issue it to the architect and/ or principal designer once appointed.	
Stage 1	**Preparation and Brief**	**Completed**
	With architect, prepare Initial Project Brief. (Refer to Chapter 6).	
	Agree project target programme.	
	Appoint other consultants as required. (This may take place in Stage 2 instead.) (Refer to Chapter 5).	
	Prepare cash flow/schedule of payments to be made through the project.	
	Review cost plan and project risk register and take any necessary action to bring these into line.	
	Agree project strategies for procurement, handover, building control and communication.	
	Select the design option that is to be developed in Stage 2 Concept Design.	
Stage 2	**Concept Design**	
	With architect, prepare Final Project Brief. (Refer to Chapter 6).	
	Review cost plan, project programme and project risk register and take any necessary action to bring into line.	
	Determine whether party wall survey/award/s needed. (Refer to Chapter 8).	
	Approve the Concept Design to be developed in Stage 3 Detailed Design. (Refer to Chapter 6).	
	Agree a change control process with the architect/ project lead.	

Stage 3	**Developed Design**	
	Review cost plan (or tenders as appropriate), project programme and project risk register and take any necessary action to bring into line.	
	Review and approve the design prior to submission for planning approval by the architect.	
Stage 4	**Technical Design**	
	With the architect/contract administrator, review tenders and appoint a contractor. (Refer to Chapter 6).	
	Take out buildings insurance if required.	
Stage 5	**Construction**	
	Give possession of the site to the contractor.	
Stage 6	**Handover and Close Out**	
	Take possession of building.	
	Inform insurers that work is complete.	
Stage 7	**In Use**	
	Instruct post-occupancy evaluation if required.	

FURTHER READING

The following documents are available, free of charge:

— *Client conversations – Insights into successful project outcome* (search online for 'RIBA client conversations')
— *RIBA Client Survey* (search 'client survey' at **www.architecture.com**)
— *Client and Architect – developing the essential relationship* (search 'client and architect' at **www.architecture.com**)
— *Party Wall etc. Act 1996 Explanatory Booklet* (download free of charge by searching for 'party wall etc. act 1996 explanatory booklet' at **www.gov.uk**)
— *CDM 2015 Industry Guidance for Clients* (download free of charge by searching for 'cdm guide for clients' at **www.citb.co.uk**).

GLOSSARY

Architect

'Architect' is a legally protected title which can only be used by people registered under the Architects Act 1997.

Architects Registration Board (ARB)

In the UK a person cannot practise or carry on a business under any name, style or title containing the word 'architect' unless they are registered with the Architects Registration Board (ARB). The list of ARB registered architects can be checked on the ARB website **www.arb.org.uk**. (See Chapter 10: ARB and RIBA codes of conduct.)

Principal contractor

Where there is more than one contractor (which is usually the case), one must be the principal contractor under the CDM Regulations 2015. The principal contractor may also take on the client's duties under the Regulations. See Chapter 7.

Principal designer

Where there will be a principal contractor there must be a principal designer under the CDM Regulations 2015. See Chapter 7.

Professional indemnity (PI) insurance

Architects must carry an appropriate amount of professional indemnity insurance. The minimum amount is £250,000 for very small practices, but the level of cover is contingent on the scale of projects the practice undertakes.

Royal Institute of British Architects (RIBA)

The Royal Institute of British Architects is a global membership body driving excellence in architecture. Founded in 1834 and awarded its Royal Charter in 1837, the RIBA is the UK charter body for architecture. The RIBA champions better buildings, communities and the environment through architecture and its members.

The RIBA also maintains a code of conduct and expects its members to work with integrity and honesty. In turn, architects will expect their clients to be honest with them and provide accurate information relating to the circumstances of their project, for example with regard to ownership rights and boundaries.

For further information visit the RIBA website **www.architecture.com**

RIBA Chartered Architects

Architects practising in the UK who are registered with the ARB and are also Chartered Members of the RIBA are entitled to describe themselves as 'Chartered Architects' and to use the suffix RIBA after their name. A directory of all Chartered Members of the RIBA is provided on the RIBA website **www.architecture.com**.

RIBA Plan of Work 2013

The Plan of Work is a framework that sets out the chronological stages to a project from start to finish. See Chapter 6: Project process.

IMAGE CREDITS

Cover photo: House No. 7, reproduced by permission of
David Barbour
The Contemporary Lean-To (p 18) images © Doma Architects
Love Shack (p 40) images © Sutherland Hussey Harris Architects